K6/15 LT 3/15

◆ DANIEL ROSEN ◆

Independence Now

The American Revolution
1763–1783

NATIONAL GEOGRAPHIC

Washington, D.C.

PICTURE CREDITS
Cover Bettmann/CORBIS; page 1 (background) Joseph Sohm/CORBIS; page 1 (borders)
Joseph Sohm, Visions of America/Corbis; pages 1 (left), 3 (bottom 2nd from left), 23
(bottom and middle) Museum of the City of New York/Corbis; pages 1 (right), 2, 3 (bottom
right), 5 (right and bottom), 9 (right), 10 (bottom and right), 12 , 13 (right), 14, 15, 16 (top
and bottom), 18, 19 (right), 22 (top), 22-23 (background), 23 (top), 25, 26, 27, 30, 31, 33,
35 (top) Bettmann/CORBIS; pages 2-7 (border) Hulton-Archive/Getty Images; pages 4
(left), 38 New York Historical Society; pages 5 (right), 11, 17 (top), 21, 22 (bottom), 33-40
(border) The Granger Collection; page 6 (bottom) Geoffrey Clements/CORBIS; page 7
Courtesy of Abby Aldrich Rockefeller Foundation, Colonial Williamsburg; page 11 Georgia
State University Library; page 17 (top) Courtesy of the Frick Art Reference Library; pages
27-31 (border) Stock Montage; pages 28-29 (bottom) Library of Congress; page 32
Giraudon/Art Resource, NY; page 34 South Carolina State Museum; page 36 United States
Postal Service; page 37 (top) Courtesy of the Danbury Historical Society.

ISBN: 0-7922-6766-4

Library of Congress Cataloging-in-Publication Data

LC Control #2003017857
Complete CIP data available on request.

Produced through the worldwide resources of the National Geographic Society, John M.
Fahey, Jr., President and Chief Executive Officer; Gilbert M. Grosvenor, Chairman of the
Board; Nina D. Hoffman, Executive Vice President and President, Books and Education
Publishing; Ericka Markman, President, Children's Books and Education Publishing Group;
Steve Mico, Vice President Education Publishing Group, Editorial Director; Marianne
Hiland, Editorial Manager; Anita Schwartz, Project Editor; Tara Peterson, Editorial Assistant;
Jim Hiscott, Design Manager; Linda McKnight, Art Director; Diana Bourdrez, Anne Whittle,
Photo Research; Matt Wascavage, Manager of Publishing Services; Sean Philpotts,
Production Coordinator; Jane Ponton, Production Artist; Susan Donnelly, Children's Books
Project Editor. Production: Clifton M. Brown III, Manufacturing and Quality Control

PROGRAM DEVELOPMENT
Gare Thompson Associates, Inc.

CONSULTANTS/REVIEWERS
Dr. Margit E. McGuire, School of Education, Seattle University, Seattle, Washington

BOOK DESIGN
Steven Curtis Design, Inc.
Maps: Sue Carlson

Published by the National Geographic Society
1145 17th Street, N.W.
Washington, D.C. 20036-4688

Printed in Mexico

Table of Contents

Benjamin Franklin

George Washington

Thomas Jefferson

John Adams

America in 1763

A CHANGING SOCIETY

The year 1763 was important for England and America. In that year, the **French and Indian War** ended. Beginning in 1754, the people of England's American **colonies** had fought alongside English soldiers against French soldiers and their Indian **allies**. They fought for control of North America, for France also had colonies there. England was the clear winner.

The war marked a change in how the English colonists saw themselves. Colonial farm boys had left their homes to fight next to young men from other colonies who were much like themselves.

Life in the colonies was changing. Roads connecting the cities were being built or improved. Trade among the colonies was growing rapidly.

People and ideas moved along with goods. Colonial newspapers looked at events from an American point of view. The colonists were shaping their own way of life.

Ships took weeks to cross the Atlantic Ocean. So the colonists had become used to governing themselves. They elected their own local representatives and made their own laws.

All these changes strengthened ties among the colonists and weakened their ties with England. Many colonists felt less *English* and more *American*.

This new sense of themselves as Americans was soon tested. England's leaders were planning some big changes for the colonies. The war against France had been expensive for England. The English thought it was fair that the colonists help pay for the war. So the English leaders passed a series of new taxes on the colonies to help pay for the war. The colonists were outraged.

ENGLISH TAX STAMP

WHO ARE THE AMERICANS?

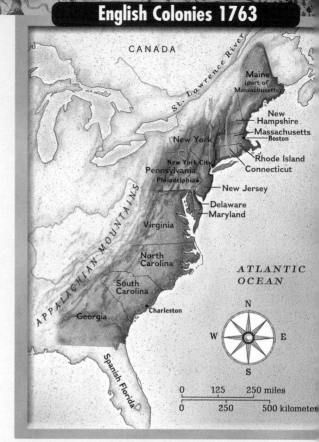

*I*n 1763, there are 13 English colonies. They stretch along the Atlantic coast of North America. English colonists had been living in North America for more than 150 years. The population has reached more than one and one half million. Who are these people?

The colonists are young. About half them are sixteen years of age or younger. They work hard. Colonists of all classes dislike idlers. In England, gentlemen prided themselves on not working at all. In the colonies, even the rich work hard.

The colonists are determined to get ahead. It is easier to move up in colonial society than it would be in England. This does not mean there is social equality in the colonies. Like the English, the colonists are divided into the rich, the middle class, and the poor. But there are fewer social barriers between one class and another. Rich colonists usually come from the middle class, and poor ones are determined to join it.

ELIJAH BOARDMAN, WHO SOLD CLOTH, SERVED IN THE AMERICAN ARMY DURING THE REVOLUTION.

A SLAVE WEDDING IN SOUTH CAROLINA

The colonists don't think the law should ever limit economic opportunity—at least for white men. But there are other barriers in colonial society. There are few economic opportunities for colonial women. They have no political power. Their lives are very limited by social customs about what is "proper" for women.

Enslaved Africans are kept at the bottom of colonial society. Free blacks have some opportunities to improve their lives. But they face many barriers too. They live apart from whites. There are black sections in large colonial cities such as New York, Boston, and Philadelphia. Free black men cannot vote. Blacks cannot testify in court against whites.

"First in war, first in peace, first in the hearts of his countrymen."

Revolutionary War hero "Light-Horse Harry" Lee, in praise of Washington

WASHINGTON GIVING ORDERS TO WORKERS AT MOUNT VERNON

CHAPTER 1

From English to American

WEDDING OF GEORGE AND MARTHA WASHINGTON

CITIZEN AND SOLDIER

One man had become a hero to the colonists. As a young officer in the French and Indian War, he proved himself a fine soldier and leader. His name was George Washington.

Washington was a quiet man. But whether in war or peace, he was somebody who people respected. Washington did not raise his voice or act important. He was a big man, usually the tallest man in the room. His manner was formal. He always acted with dignity. Both the men he led in the army and his neighbors in Virginia looked up to him.

Washington left the army in 1758. He returned to Mount Vernon, his Virginia **plantation**.

Washington loved his life there. He took an active hand in every part of plantation life. He was very interested in raising fine cattle and horses.

Washington also enjoyed a busy social life. He and his wife Martha often held parties and dances at Mount Vernon. Washington was a fine horseman. One of his favorite pastimes was riding in foxhunts.

Like many colonists, Washington did not like the changing English attitude towards the colonies. Even with the peace, he was aware that the colonies faced new challenges. Washington often wrote to friends about his happiness in being retired from army life. He did not know that the biggest battles still lay ahead, both for him and his country.

A TERRIBLE TAX

In 1765, the English government passed the **Stamp Act**. It was one of a series of taxes on the colonies to pay for England's wars with France. The Stamp Act forced colonists to buy special stamps for paper products, such as newspapers, legal documents, marriage licenses—even playing cards.

Many colonists were furious! They organized protests and wrote articles against the tax. They claimed that the new tax violated their rights. The colonists argued that they had not elected the English government. To be taxed without a voice was unfair.

The protests took England's leaders by surprise. They thought the tax made sense. But with so much protest, the English backed down and withdrew the Stamp Act.

ENGLISH TAX STAMPS

The protests against the Stamp Act had an important effect. Before the Stamp Act, the colonies did not agree with one another about many issues. But the Stamp Act gave the colonists a common enemy. They began to work together to oppose English taxes.

When England imposed more taxes, colonists found new ways to protest. They refused to buy English goods. In New York, a young woman named Charity Clark joined the protests. She was one of hundreds of colonial women who met together to spin wool rather than buy English thread.

MERCY OTIS WARREN OF MASSACHUSETTS URGED COLONIAL WOMEN NOT TO BUY ENGLISH GOODS.

"Heroines may not distinguish themselves at the head of an army, but freedom will also be won by a fighting army of women armed with spinning wheels."

Charity Clark, in a letter to an English friend, 1769

STAMP ACT PROTEST

ENGLISH SOLDIERS FIRING
AT COLONISTS

THE BOSTON MASSACRE

In 1770, conflict between the colonists and the English turned deadly. The governor of Massachusetts requested troops be sent from England to restore order. People in Boston were very angry that English soldiers were stationed in their city.

On the cold afternoon of March 5, 1770, a crowd gathered and began to taunt a group of English soldiers. Among them was Crispus Attucks, a large, powerful dockworker who was part African and part Native American. He carried a big stick, and he used it to knock one of the soldiers down. Someone yelled, "Fire!" and the guns went off. When the smoke cleared, Attucks and two others were dead. Two wounded colonists died later that night.

The event became known as the "Boston Massacre." The city was ready to explode. The governor knew he had to act, so he arrested the soldiers. The next day, 34-year-old John Adams was asked to defend them. No one else would take the case.

COLONISTS WERE OUTRAGED BY THIS PICTURE OF THE BOSTON MASSACRE.

Adams was a Massachusetts farmer's son. He spoke his mind frankly, enjoyed a good argument, and had a great sense of humor. Adams was a brilliant lawyer and a serious student of government. He was known as a fair and honest man. During the trial, Adams argued that the soldiers had fired because they feared they were going to be attacked.

The jury found two of the soldiers guilty and cleared the others. People in Boston were satisfied with the verdict. But tension between the English king and the colonists continued to grow.

THE BOSTON TEA PARTY

Life in the colonies was more peaceful after the Boston Massacre. That changed in 1773. Once more, Boston was the center of protest. Colonists were upset about a new tax on tea, their favorite drink. Before 1773, colonial merchants controlled the sale of tea. But a new law gave that control to an English company. This meant higher prices for tea.

In December 1773, three English ships loaded with tea arrived in Boston Harbor. Colonists called a meeting to spread the word.

After the meeting, 50 or 60 men disguised as Mohawk Indians marched to the docks. The "Indians" rowed out into the harbor and boarded each ship. Then they dumped every crate of tea they could find into the harbor, some 45 tons of tea. On shore, a large crowd of Boston's citizens cheered the men on.

The Boston Tea Party enraged King George III of England. At the king's orders, the English government passed even harsher laws against the colonies. The new laws alarmed the colonists. People who had been happy with English rule now joined together in opposing the king.

COLONISTS DISGUISED AS INDIANS ROWING OUT TO ENGLISH SHIPS IN BOSTON HARBOR

MOVING TOWARD INDEPENDENCE

Colonial leaders were divided. Some favored continuing to search for a peaceful solution to the colonists' conflicts with England. In 1774, George Washington wrote to a friend that he supported the protests against England. But, he added, "No thinking man in North America supports full independence."

Patrick Henry did not agree with him. Henry was a lawyer from Virginia. In 1765, he had given a fiery speech against the Stamp Act. In March 1775, ten years later, he delivered another speech that was to go down in history. Henry said it was time to prepare for war against England.

Americans began to be divided into two groups over the question of independence. Those who favored breaking with England were known as **Patriots**. Those who favored staying with England were known as **Loyalists** or **Tories**.

IN THEIR OWN WORDS

"Gentlemen may cry, peace, peace—but there is no peace. The war is actually begun! Is life so dear, or peace so sweet, as to be purchased at the price of chains and slavery! I know not what course others may take; but as for me, give me liberty or give me death!"

Patrick Henry

Should America Be Independent?

The debate over whether America should be independent sometimes divided families. Benjamin Franklin, the famous American writer, scientist, and statesman, was a Patriot leader. His son William, the last royal governor of the colony of New Jersey, was a Loyalist.

Benjamin Franklin believed that English society was corrupt and that the Americans should break away. He also felt that what the Americans were fighting for was greater than just their own freedom.

*W*hen I consider the extreme corruption among all orders of men in this old rotten state [England], and the glorious public virtue in our rising country, I cannot but see more mischief than benefit from a closer union.

It is a common observation [in France] that our cause is the cause of all mankind, and that we are fighting for their liberty in defending our own.

PATRIOTS SAW ENGLISH SOLDIERS AS MURDERERS IN THE BOSTON MASSACRE

As royal governor, William Franklin felt that he must remain loyal to his king, George III. He believed that the Patriot leaders would drag the colonies into a horrible civil war. He also felt that the American people themselves did not at heart support the Patriot cause.

You have now pointed out to you, gentlemen [New Jersey's colonial leaders], *two roads—one clearly leading to peace, happiness and a restoration of the public order—the other certainly conducting you to lawlessness, misery, and all the horrors of a civil war.*

LOYALISTS SAW MOB RULE IN ATTACKS ON ENGLISH OFFICIALS

Were the People, even now, left to judge for themselves, I have no doubt but their natural good sense would prevent their engaging in the support of the present hostile and destructive measures.

The conflict between Benjamin Franklin and his son reflected the one between Patriots and Loyalists throughout the colonies. The American Revolution was, in one sense, a civil war.

THE BATTLE OF LEXINGTON

The War Begins

PAUL REVERE'S RIDE

LEXINGTON AND CONCORD

On the night of April 18, 1775, Paul Revere stared up at the spire of Old North Church in Boston. He was waiting for a signal. Revere was a member of the **Minutemen**, the Patriot **militia**. These were citizen soldiers ready to respond "at a minute's warning." The signal was to be one lantern if the English were marching overland or two lanterns if they were sailing up the river. Two lanterns appeared in the church tower. Revere jumped on his horse and set out for the nearby towns of Lexington and Concord. Along the way, he rode past the houses of the Minutemen, calling a warning into the night, "The British are coming!"

A column of red-coated English soldiers marched through the dark night toward Concord to capture a storehouse of Patriots' weapons. At dawn, they reached Lexington.

Thanks to Revere, a force of 70 Minutemen was waiting for them there. The English commander ordered the Americans to lay down their guns and leave. Before they could do so, shots were fired. No one knows by whom. Then the English soldiers fired on the Minutemen. Eight Americans were killed, and ten more were wounded. The English marched on to Concord. The English searched for the weapons, but the colonists had moved most of them.

A few hours later, the English started back to Boston. But now the trip was deadly. The time the English spent in Concord had allowed more Minutemen to arrive and hide behind stone walls and fences along the road. The bright red coats of the English made them easy targets for the Minutemen. War had really begun.

THE BATTLE OF BUNKER HILL

Two months later, another battle took place near Boston. The Minutemen were camped north of the city. An English force set out to attack them. The Americans had an advantage because they were on high ground. But they were badly outnumbered and had little ammunition.

The Patriots let the English get very close. Then they opened fire. Hundreds of red-coated soldiers fell dead and wounded. Twice the English retreated. The third time they advanced, the Patriots ran out of ammunition. They had to retreat. The English won the battle, but at great cost. And the Patriots had shown they could hold their own against the most powerful army in the world.

The Patriots knew they had to prepare to fight a war. Their representatives met at a **Continental Congress** in Philadelphia to organize an army. At John Adams' urging, the Congress appointed George Washington Commander in Chief of the American army.

Washington was the perfect leader for the army. He was brave to the point of recklessness. He respected his men, which won him their undying loyalty and admiration. His earlier wartime experiences had taught him how the English fought.

Washington also understood that the colonists did not need to win every battle to win the war. He believed that he simply had to outlast the English to win. The longer the war continued, the more likely the people in England would tire of it.

BATTLE OF BUNKER HILL

Paintings

"He was incapable of fear," Patriot leader Thomas Jefferson said of George Washington. Called the "Father of His Country," Washington was the first American hero. These paintings show his strength as a soldier and leader, his love for his family, and his faith in God.

WASHINGTON CROSSING THE DELAWARE, BY EMANUEL GOTTLIEB LEUTZE

WASHINGTON'S FAMILY, BY EDWARD SAVAGE

GEORGE WASHINGTON AT THE
BATTLE OF PRINCETON,
BY CHARLES WILLSON PEALE

GEORGE WASHINGTON,
BY GILBERT STUART

THE DECLARATION OF INDEPENDENCE

As 1776 began, most Americans still hoped for peace with England. That changed quickly, mostly due to a little book by Thomas Paine called *Common Sense*. Paine argued that the cause of liberty could only be served by independence. His book sold like hotcakes. In just a few short months, *Common Sense* changed how most Americans felt about separating from England.

The Continental Congress appointed a small committee to write a statement of independence. The committee included John Adams, Benjamin Franklin, and Thomas Jefferson. Franklin was probably the most famous man in the colonies. Jefferson was born into a wealthy Virginia family. He was polite and soft-spoken. Like Adams, he was a lawyer who read widely and thought deeply about government. Franklin and Adams asked Jefferson to write the statement of independence. His abilities as a thinker and writer were well known.

When Jefferson showed his work to Adams and Franklin, they made only a few small changes. On July 4, 1776, the Continental Congress voted in favor of the Declaration of Independence.

Now the Patriots were no longer fighting to win agreements from King George. They were fighting for independence. The Declaration of Independence was printed and sent to every colony. In each town, it was read, discussed, and argued about. Most people were in favor of independence. But many Loyalists still opposed separating from England. Those who spoke out were often beaten and chased out of town by Patriot neighbors. Many Loyalists left and moved to Canada.

IN THEIR OWN WORDS

"We hold these truths to be self evident: that all men are created equal."

Thomas Jefferson, Declaration of Independence

FRANKLIN, ADAMS, AND JEFFERSON WORKING ON THE DECLARATION OF INDEPENDENCE

"We must all hang together or, assuredly, we will all hang separately."

Benjamin Franklin

AMERICANS PULLING DOWN A STATUE OF KING GEORGE III

CHAPTER 3

The Best and Worst of Times

GEORGE WASHINGTON AND AMERICAN TROOPS

A POWERFUL ENEMY

Now America was officially at war with England. The Patriot leaders were taking a huge risk. If they lost the war, the English would probably hang them.

At this time, the chances of an American victory seemed small. England was just too powerful. This chart compares the strengths and weaknesses of England and America.

England	America
STRENGTHS	**STRENGTHS**
• More soldiers	• Fighting on home soil
• Best trained army in the world	• Fighting for a cause
• Experienced officers	• Leadership of Washington and other officers
• Strongest navy in the world	• Fine marksmanship
• More supplies	
WEAKNESSES	**WEAKNESSES**
• Fighting far from home	• Unprofessional, poorly trained army
• Soldiers less committed to victory	• Lack of supplies
	• Small navy

ENGLISH PLAN FOR VICTORY

In 1777, the English put together a plan that would have won the war if it had been successful. The plan was simple. General William Howe would march up the Hudson River Valley towards Albany. General John Burgoyne would march south from Montreal. And Colonel Barry St. Leger would march east from Lake Ontario. The three armies would meet in Albany. They would then have cut New England off from the rest of the colonies.

It was a wonderful plan, but it didn't work. General Howe changed his mind. Instead of marching north to Albany, he turned south and marched to Philadelphia. Colonel St. Leger made it about halfway across New York. Then he was defeated by American soldiers and forced to turn back.

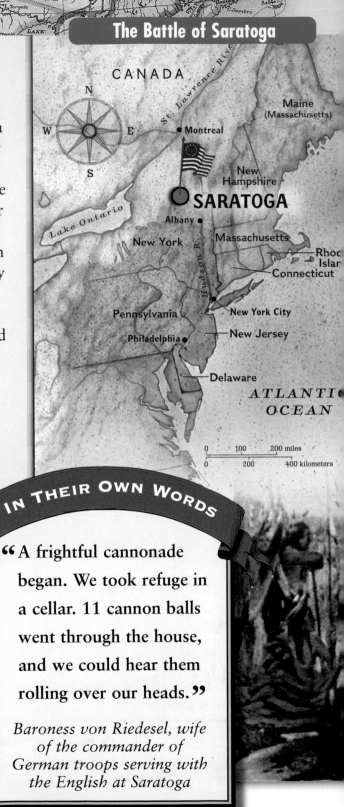

The Battle of Saratoga

IN THEIR OWN WORDS

"A frightful cannonade began. We took refuge in a cellar. 11 cannon balls went through the house, and we could hear them rolling over our heads."

Baroness von Riedesel, wife of the commander of German troops serving with the English at Saratoga

28

THE TURNING POINT

"Gentleman Johnny," as Burgoyne was known, had success at first. He captured Fort Ticonderoga on Lake Champlain. But when General Burgoyne reached Saratoga, New York, he was attacked by the American army led by General Horatio Gates. Much to Burgoyne's surprise, the Americans drove his troops back.

Burgoyne retreated, waiting for the armies of Howe and St. Leger. But soon, Burgoyne's scouts brought him the dreadful news. Howe and St. Leger were not coming.

Burgoyne made one final attempt to break through the American lines, but was driven back. By now, Burgoyne was outnumbered. His men were running out of food and ammunition. Burgoyne realized he was defeated. On October 17, 1777, he surrendered his entire army.

The victory at Saratoga changed the outcome of the war. Benjamin Franklin had been in France, trying to get the French to come into the war on the Patriot side. He had faced a tough task. When the French heard about Saratoga, they decided to enter the war. The French realized that the Americans might actually win!

GENERAL BURGOYNE SURRENDERING AT SARATOGA

29

A HARD WINTER

With the victory at Saratoga, the winter of 1777–1778 should have been a happy one for the Americans. Instead, it was the hardest time of the war. Washington's soldiers were low on food and supplies. The Continental Congress had a hard time raising money.

In the 1700s, armies did not fight in the wintertime. It was too hard to move troops in the snow and ice. Washington decided to take his army to Valley Forge, Pennsylvania, for the winter. Valley Forge was near Philadelphia. That way, Washington could keep an eye on Howe's English army in Philadelphia.

Unfortunately for the Americans, the winter of 1777–1778 was bitterly cold. Early snow and brutally cold temperatures settled in before the army had a chance to build shelters. There were shortages of food and clothing. Boots wore out. Men wrapped their feet in cloth to walk through the snow.

The conditions at Valley Forge were worse for the men than any battle. The men slept on straw mats in drafty, cold cabins. Their main meal was a mixture of flour and water called "firecake." Of the ten thousand men who marched into Valley Forge that winter, more than two thousand died.

Washington spent the winter trying to get his army ready to fight. Baron von Steuben was a German general. He had come to America to help in the fight for freedom. Washington put Baron von Steuben in charge of training the army. He held drills all through the winter. The men worked hard, even though they could hardly understand what the German general was saying.

BARON VON STEUBEN

"December 14th—Poor food—hard lodging—cold weather—I can't endure it—why are we sent here to starve and freeze?"

Diary of Albigence Waldo, surgeon with the American army at Valley Forge

WASHINGTON AT VALLEY FORGE

"Oh God, it's all over!"

*English leader Lord North,
on hearing that Cornwallis
had surrendered*

THE BATTLE OF YORKTOWN

CHAPTER 4

Fighting On

A LONG WAY TO VICTORY

CORNWALLIS SURRENDERS TO WASHINGTON

In 1779, the English turned their attention to the Southern colonies. They captured the important cities of Savannah, Georgia, and Charleston, South Carolina. George Washington got tired of the defeats. He replaced General Gates, the hero of Saratoga, with General Nathanael Greene. The Americans began to have success.

The English commander, General Cornwallis, decided to move his army to Yorktown on the Virginia coast. He expected the English navy to bring troops and supplies by ship to Yorktown.

George Washington saw a chance to end the war. But he had to act quickly! He came up with a plan. By this time, French troops and warships had arrived to help the Americans.

Washington's army and the French forces of General Rochambeau would join American troops led by the French general Marquis de Lafayette. The French fleet of warships would sail quickly to Yorktown. The land forces would surround Cornwallis, making escape by land impossible. The French fleet would stop the English from landing more troops or escaping by sea.

In September 1781, Cornwallis saw French ships off the coast. His scouts brought news of the approach of Washington, Rochambeau, and Lafayette. The English tried to fight their way out, but they were surrounded and outnumbered. Cornwallis saw that the situation was hopeless, so he surrendered his army to Washington.

AFRICAN AMERICANS IN THE REVOLUTION

What role had African Americans played in the Revolution? The English invited those who were slaves to desert their masters and join the English forces. They promised freedom to those who would fight. Many joined the English and fought against the Patriots. When the English troops left at the end of the war, thousands of African Americans left with them.

But many African Americans fought for the Patriots too. At first, George Washington and other Patriot leaders did not allow African Americans to serve in the army. They doubted their loyalty to a country that had enslaved them, and they feared to arm them.

But Washington needed soldiers very badly. So he changed his mind. By the end of the war, at least 5,000 African Americans had served in the American army. Many fought bravely and won their freedom through army service.

AN AFRICAN-AMERICAN SOLDIER SHOOTING AT ENGLISH CAVALRY DURING A BATTLE IN SOUTH CAROLINA IN 1781

WOMEN IN THE REVOLUTION

Life in the Patriot army was very different from modern armies. Many soldiers brought their wives and families along. The most famous of these camp women was probably Martha Washington, George's wife. The army did not have nurses, cooks, or people to sew and repair uniforms. Women did those tasks. And a few women actually fought alongside the soldiers.

George Washington honored one woman for her brave service. On a terribly hot day, Mary Hays carried a pitcher of water to the fighting men. When her husband was wounded, she helped load the cannon so it could continue firing. The soldiers called her "Molly Pitcher."

But most women stayed at home. They ran the family farms and businesses while the men were away. Abigail Adams, John's wife, ran the family farm for years.

MOLLY PITCHER

IN THEIR OWN WORDS

"In the new code of laws, I desire you would remember the ladies. Do not put such unlimited power into the hands of husbands. Remember all men would be tyrants if they could."

Abigail Adams

SYBIL LUDINGTON'S MIDNIGHT RIDE

Sybil Ludington was a 16-year-old girl in 1777. Her father was commander of the local militia in the area around Danbury, Connecticut. As the eldest daughter, Sybil helped care for her many young brothers and sisters. One rainy night, a messenger knocked on the door. The English were attacking Danbury. Colonel Ludington had to gather the local militia he commanded. But his men were at their homes scattered over many miles. Colonel Ludington had to stay to organize the men. But Sybil knew where all the men lived.

Sybil pleaded with her father to let her go. She was an excellent rider and knew the area well. Colonel Ludington didn't want to send Sybil on such a dangerous mission. But he realized he had no choice. He helped her saddle her horse, Star, and went over the route she should take.

Sybil took off at a full gallop. She picked up a long stick to use for banging on doors. It would save getting off Star at each house. She rode up to each house, banged on the door with her stick, and shouted, "The British are burning Danbury! Gather at Ludington's!"

POSTAGE STAMP HONORING SYBIL LUDINGTON

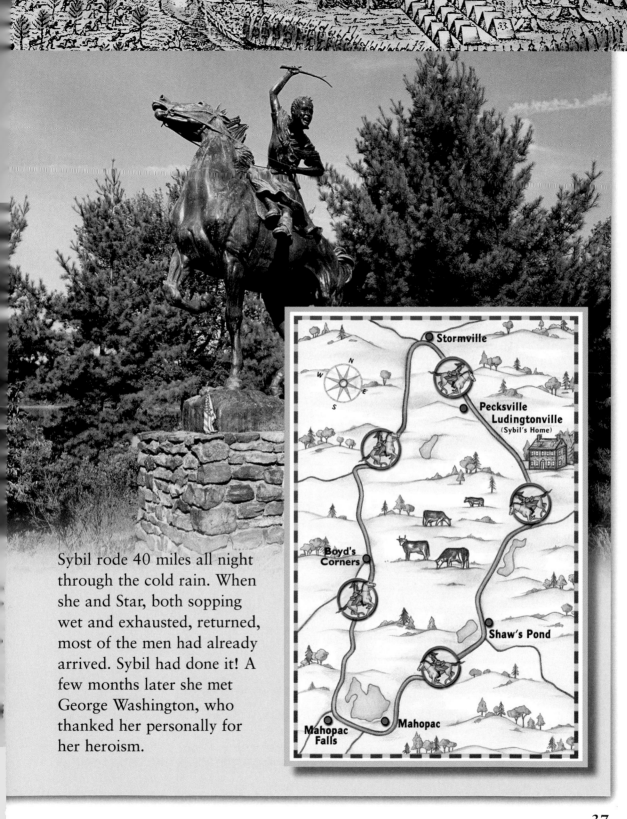

Sybil rode 40 miles all night through the cold rain. When she and Star, both sopping wet and exhausted, returned, most of the men had already arrived. Sybil had done it! A few months later she met George Washington, who thanked her personally for her heroism.

Stormville

Pecksville
Ludingtonville
(Sybil's Home)

Boyd's
Corners

Shaw's Pond

Mahopac
Falls

Mahopac

Legacy

England and America signed the **Treaty of Paris** in 1783. The war was over. The 13 English colonies had become the United States of America, an independent nation. The cost had been high. The eight years of fighting had taken a terrible toll. Over 25,000 Americans died in the war. Many returning soldiers had no money. Thousands of Loyalists had lost their property. Many left the United States. Most went to Canada.

But the Patriot victory changed human history. For as Benjamin Franklin had observed, the cause the Americans were fighting for was bigger than their own freedom. They had "fired a shot heard round the world." In the years that followed, people in many places would be inspired by the American Revolution to seek to win their own independence.

Glossary

ALLY people or country that supports another people or country in war

COLONY territory ruled by a foreign government

CONTINENTAL CONGRESS Patriot governing body that signed the Declaration of Independence and formed the American army

FRENCH AND INDIAN WAR war fought from 1754 to 1763 between England and France for control of North America

LOYALIST American colonist who supported staying a part of England

MINUTEMEN Patriot militia trained to respond "at a minute's warning"

MILITIA an army of citizens who are not professional soldiers

PATRIOT American colonist who favored independence

PLANTATION a large farm on which crops are raised, often by workers who live on the plantation

STAMP ACT tax law passed in 1765 by England that forced American colonists to buy special stamps for paper products

TORY another name for a Loyalist

TREATY OF PARIS treaty signed in 1783 by England and America that ended the Revolutionary War

Index